Forward:

A Pragmatic Agenda

KAI TIMMERMANN

Printed in the United States of America

First Printing, 2018

ISBN 978-0-9975035-2-4

Folino Media
64 Blazier Road
Martinsville NJ 08836

www.FolinoMedia.com

For Irene

KAI TIMMERMANN

Fôrwərd

adverb — onward so as to make progress; toward a successful conclusion

adjective — relating to or concerned with the future

verb — help to advance (something); promote

-Google.com

KAI TIMMERMANN

Table of Contents

KAI TIMMERMANN

Preface

We have work to do.

We need to re-orient the political climate towards clarity and outcomes instead of generalities, hyperbole, dogma, demagoguery, over-simplification, false certainty or the promise of a nostalgic return to some yesteryear that neither exists nor is relevant.

We face real, complex issues in which our federal government plays a critical part. Denying those issues adequate media or air-time or relegating the federal government to an ineffective zombie or reality entertainment is neither helpful nor practical. Untangling the issues and dealing with the necessary ones requires careful thinking, direct civil conversation, deliberate choices, and sustained, structural action.

This book is a proposed Pragmatic Agenda for the United States' federal government describing the priorities to move forward.

It is framed, very intentionally, in different language. In so doing, I also hope to convey the importance — and possibilities — of choice and action — and getting beyond talk and rousing a base and get to results.

It is specific rather than surface-political. It can be hard to have a successful constructive discussion in our current climate without specifics. Labels — like liberal, conservative, Democrat or Republican — are slippery. As an example, 'conservative' can be used in a variety of meanings including small federal government, religious / spiritual social footing and/or 'free market' capitalism. So, I will intentionally do my best to avoid labels.

My intent is directness, clarity and essence rather than emotional appeal: applying light to the key problems that need to be addressed (and how) rather than heat.

And, of course, trying my best to walk the fine line between over-simplifying and over-complicating.

Is Pragmatism Idealistic?

The paradox at the heart of framing this book as a pragmatic approach is best captured in a statement by a friend as we talked through some of the contents: "They (the current Legislative and Executive Branch members) will never do that. It's not in their interests."

Implying that my belief that pragmatism could create a path forward is, at its core, idealistic.

Yes and no.

"Yes" in the sense that I am quite aware that what I am suggesting involves significant change — driven from the electorate. I believe, for example, that we need term limits in Congress. And I am not bullish that Congress will do that without voters pushing for it.

"No" in that discussions I've had over the past year with folks from a variety of political persuasions suggest to me that pragmatism bridges the differences well — even in our current emotional land-mine fraught political state.

By no means does everyone like or agree with every policy. And there are thornier areas where disagreements will simply exist regardless. But pragmatism, as captured throughout this book, presents a foundation to talk, resolve and act to move forward.

Digressions

Finally, there are points in the book where I break with the narrative and dive into how I believe pragmatism – as a system – needs to work to be successful.

Perspective

Before launching into the book, a brief word about my background as it may help inform you of my perspective, why I choose to weigh-in, and why you should read on.

Maybe it takes an outsider to call attention to the seemingly obvious.

Getting things done and creating constructive environments that perform has been my role as a business executive for thirty plus years in operations, technology and strategy.

It's important for leadership to understand the Big Picture — where things are, where they are going, selecting where to go and key specific steps to get there — yet there will always be more knowledgeable folks in certain areas.

Understanding the impact of technology strategically (e.g., how it changes how value is distributed in industry and the economy) and tactically (e.g., understanding importance of getting upstream / reference data correct, delivering information at right time and format to create the targeted behavior) is also critical— yet cutting through the hyperbole within the rapidly changing environment means relying on those exposed to it daily to sort fact from fiction.

Leadership obviously matters also — articulating a path, prioritizing the agenda, selecting the order of the needed actions, demonstrating a positive track record, dealing with adversity, face-to-face interaction to engage and explain, etc.

But, in the end, however, success has always involved engaging the array of stakeholders in an upright and authentic manner and aiming at a shared objective.

Much of my professional background has been within supply chain / logistics — where there must be both agreement to optimize the end-result as well as constant awareness and communications upstream and downstream. All participants have their specific needs but if you opt to skip a step for a personal benefit, ramifications downstream can be significant.

As a third-party logistics provider — meaning we provide the distribution and transportation services for product that isn't ours — we are always working with our customers, potentially their vendors and mindful of potential end-consumers — meshing their needs and expectations with our own and the final outcome. Multi-constituent conditions are normal in business but to succeed they must be clear, mutually beneficial, and based upon agreed necessary outcomes.

Implementing change is always about engaging the team — not only getting people on-board with where you are going (meaning gaining consensus and buy-in through face-to-face discussion and explanation) — but also in data-gathering both up-front (e.g., input to help gather information, identify systemically critical details and potential pitfalls) and during the process (to learn/ adjust to new information).

Oftentimes it has meant bringing in those most opposed to — or skeptical of — the targeted change and *really* listening to understand their views and concerns (as opposed to simply doing it for the optics). Sometimes you hear a new fact or a new perspective that changes the path or adds a layer.

There's no doubt in my mind that we have work to do and getting there involves bridging excess partisanship through a focus on outcomes, teamwork and Pragmatism as the foundation and frame by which to move forward.

Enjoy.

Foundation

The Pragmatic Agenda is founded on Principles — what we want to be — and Law — rules of the road.

The **Principles** root in the US national story and highlight qualities that reflect what the US is about and — importantly — what's worked:

> Principle 1. Defend the spirit of individual liberties and aspirations - as diverse as they may be - and equal opportunities.

> Principle 2. Develop and harness the strengths, opportunities and dynamism created by our heterogeneous culture.

> Principle 3. Understand the United States' responsibility and role to be a constructive force in the world.

> Principle 4. Government must be by the people and for the people.

> Principle 5. Assess ideas and policies based on current data, realized outcomes, practical evidence, and clarified objectives.

That simple.

Let's break it down further:

There's originalism: explicit grounding in the Declaration of Independence and the Constitution and extending to paraphrase President Lincoln's Gettysburg Address.

There's adaptive realism: the world has become increasingly interdependent and the United States plays a key lead role on the world stage and is significantly impacted by it. The diverse, multicultural character of our population, and the need to come to terms with how to both accommodate and leverage that diversity as a strength, is critical. We rely on immigration to support key aspects of our economy from agriculture to hospitality services to technology and R&D sectors.

There's idealism: embedded within the Principles above is a re-commitment to the National Project. Not to romanticize the narrative, but the United States was founded on an essential ideal and, at our best, has lived up to those ideals.

There's both ardent individualism and appreciation of the importance of community. The former explicit, the latter implied, but critical.

It is unabashedly about equalizing opportunities and intentionally not necessarily outcomes. We cannot ignore unequal outcomes as they directly affect opportunities presented to the next generation, but unequal outcomes send messages about areas of necessary focus. Nevertheless, the objective is on level-setting opportunities regardless of socio-economic, genetic or geographic backdrop.

It incorporates and harnesses differences. While there may be much to agree on, there is certainly much we won't. And shouldn't. Not everyone will reach the same conclusion with the same data (a good thing). Allowing space for difference, framework for discussion about what we *essentially* want and *really* know, and a mindset that allows compromise must be part of the solution.

The Law frames how we can operate. I am no lawyer; however, the US Constitution provides a good starting point for understanding how the federal government ought to act — and by which it should be constrained.

I include some of the key relevant articles in the Appendix, but several points worth calling out:

- The US Constitution's essential intent distributing power between state v federal entities and executive branch v legislative seems clear. As does the rules regarding what needs to happen to amend the Constitution.
- Separating and delineating the roles of the various branches governs power through (a) checks and balances among the federal branches and (b) carving out specifically named responsibilities for the federal level while keeping others local and accessible to citizens. Technology modernizes the dynamics of how it can work yet the importance of that basic governance structure and principles remain.
- The Amendments to the US Constitution capture and enshrine rights as agreed by the two-thirds designated in Article V. Of course, articles XIII, XV and XIX are 'right' — but their very existence underscores the importance of the legislative branch ante-ing up and doing its job to craft law rather than leaving it to the courts or executive edicts.

The Foundation — comprised of both the Principles and the Law — is important to internalize as both are at the core and set the boundary of what follows.

Specifically note the logical AND condition — meaning that all persons "are created equal that they are endowed by their Creator with certain unalienable

Rights, that among these are Life, Liberty and the pursuit of Happiness" AND the specifically limited role of federal government.

They coexist. It's not one or the other.

Pragmatic Agenda

The previously listed Principles outline our core national values; the Law dictates how the federal government can act. This book's proposed Agenda is the needed course of action given our current circumstances. It needs to be finite. Concrete. Systemically comprehensive. Robust.

In broad strokes:

- **Revitalize economic opportunity** through increasing economic dynamism and representative capitalism.
- **Rebuild civic dynamics** through delivering on the responsibilities implied by the freedom of speech and emphasizing both reciprocity and actuality.
- **Focus foreign and defense policy** mindful to select critical interests and incorporate macro changes.
- **Address structural flaws in federal government** emphasizing representative-ness and operational performance.

None of these are simple nor a one-step cure-all.

What I propose are the priority areas of focus, core design principles to work to and first steps towards moving our nation forward.

All involve large-scale, complicated systems with a host of participants and stakeholders with varied motivations who will adjust their behavior over time and under different conditions. Refinement and adjustments will be necessary, but it is critical to have the foundation understood as a steady point of reference.

But one thing is absolutely certain — we need to go forward.

So let's break the components down.

Digression — Representative Capitalism

It's beyond dispute that capitalism — by which I mean an economic system including private ownership of means of production and fundamental profit motive — has successfully moved the world forward, pulling people out of poverty and advancing standards of living.

There are different flavors or degrees of capitalism — depending upon objectives and socio- or political trajectories — with different degrees of state involvement and outcomes.

In the US, there's been recent soul searching regarding capitalism given issues of increasing inequality, sluggish growth and the generally held perception that things are getting harder: is the system working or does it need an overhaul of sorts?

There's been suggestions of moral, ethical, or fair capitalism – but I lean away from those concepts. They are to a large extent subjective and capitalism is, by definition, a distributed set of decisions and, therefore, what might be perceived as fair or ethical by one participant may not be to another. So difficult to assess.

Balanced capitalism appears more objective but has two issues: like 'fair' it is based on the outcome rather than the mechanism so, again, difficult to assess. More importantly, part of why capitalism works is that its core dynamic uses inequality in supply and demand – through prices – to shift behavior. Or more concretely a business with greater profits should rightfully attract more competition / capital. The lack of balance induces the behavior you're trying to create.

Instead my touchstone is upstream — "representative capitalism" — meaning if you consider a particular decision point in a capitalist economic system, to what degree does it represent the entire range of stakeholders and to what extent does it refresh?

This is not simply about diversity in management. Yes, assessing whether business management represents the population from racial, gender, religious or sexuality points of view is important, but it is limited. Representative capitalism also considers socio-economic aspects and geography and is not simply about management but also at deeper organizational points where key decisions are made (where to locate, where to allocate capital, who to fund).

And this has a time component – to what extent does representation change over time? You want a healthy amount of changeover. You want new perspectives. You want new memes and germs of new ideas and innovation to get involved.

What we are seeing in industry consolidation, reduced business formation, increased wealth inequality, and reduced lending by commercial banks to small and mid-sized businesses all point to lower underlying representative-ness in the economic system.

Finally – and critically — representative capitalism is not a description of end-state but rather a tool: it is clearly not socialism nor eliminating income disparity for reasons I mentioned earlier – but rather a mindset for policy-makers and government to use when crafting policy and a framework to look at the decisions that go into funding and key business decisions (where to create, who to employ, etc.) and how decision-makers represents the populace.

Differences in income and return send signals that drive decisions in the market and by participants based on the profit motive. Distorting or blurring those signals — even if positively intended —may not be a good thing.

Representative capitalism is simply about ensuring the broadest range of views are included and new views are introduced over time.

Part I — Revitalize Economic Opportunity

The economic world has changed; you don't need to look far to see the issues:

- Automation and technology have — and will continue to — disrupt / destroy many traditional jobs.
- Global trade and price deflation, driven by market forces including competition, may be a good thing for consumers but, again, creates disruption.
- Many reports cite labor shortages — both in skilled jobs in manufacturing and tech as well as seasonal low-paying jobs such as agriculture and services.
- Growth of labor productivity in the US has slowed drastically — to 0.4% over the 2011— 2015 period vs the 2.3% since the 1950s.
- According to data from the Federal Reserve, millennials are earning 20% less that baby boomers at the same stage of life, have half the net worth of boomers and lower home ownership.
- Disruption has had uneven effects — concentrating wealth for some and, for those at the sharp end of the decisions / disruptions, making achieving their economic objectives that much harder.
- Net rate of new business creation has been negative since the Great Recession. Per a 2017 study from the Economic Innovation Group:

    Prior to 2008, the vast majority of metro areas— at least 80 percent—saw more firms open than close in any given year, including recessions. The Great Recession completely inverted this trend, with only 11 percent of metro areas adding firms in 2009. Even in 2014, five years into the recovery, three out of five metro areas were still shedding firms.... The deficit in new firms significantly harms the labor market, muting both the quality and quantity of job growth since the recession ended. For example, the economy would have produced 924,000 additional jobs in new companies in 2014 alone had the startup rate been as high as in 2006. Historically, new companies create an average of 2.9 million jobs per year, while established companies tend to be net job destroyers.

- Despite widely cited disruption, concentration of markets to older firms has increased.

  Companies at least 16 years old are increasingly dominant in U.S. industry with nearly three out of every four American workers on their payrolls in 2014. The four largest firms now capture at least 25 percent of the market in nearly half of U.S. industries. Meanwhile, corporate profits have climbed to a record 9.4 percent of GDP.... Historically, new companies create an average of 2.9 million jobs per year, while established companies tend to be net job destroyers.

Against this back-drop — and understanding the federal government's role is primarily indirect - the essential lift for the federal government must be to spur economic dynamism and representative capitalism.

How do we get there from here?

Speak to a path of economic growth

It should be no surprise that the Agenda starts with revitalizing the economy and that the first item is about speaking to a path of growth — how we feel about the economy and the future opportunities heavily influences how we act.

Potential security-related considerations regarding food, energy, defense and technology sectors aside, it is not for the federal government to mind specific businesses.

But setting a broader vision of economic growth is. Specifically, a vision that shifts capital and attention from advertising-driven applications and social media that dominated much of the last two decades and towards both increasing productivity in service sectors and driving new frontiers and markets.

That statement requires some unpacking and explanation.

Two Productivities – Bounded and Macroeconomic

Back in 1987 Nobel Prize winning economist Robert Solow quipped "what everyone feels to have been a technological revolution, a drastic change in our productive lives, has been accompanied everywhere … by a slowing-down of productivity growth, not by a step up. You can see the computer age everywhere but in the productivity statistics."[1]

His reference was to the apparent disconnect between significant computer investment on one hand with the expectation of economic benefits and a slow-down in productivity.

We're at a similar moment now. According to the Bureau of Labor Statistics, despite omnipresent technical innovation, labor productivity growth during this business cycle is the lowest since 1948: an overall average of 2.3% with a recent high of about 2.7% between 2001 and 2007 and since 2007 at an average of 1.1%[2].

---

[1] "We'd Better Watch Out", New York Times, July 12 1987

[2] https://www.bls.gov/opub/btn/volume-6/below-trend-the-us-productivity-slowdown-since-the-great-recession.htm

The paradox at the heart of productivity lies in dual uses of the word — and the disconnect between the meanings:

- In a bounded sense — meaning within a firm or a sector, productivity is about quantity output per a given input.
- In a macroeconomic sense — looking economy wide — the sense of the word remains the same, but the specific meaning is different. In this use, productivity is gross domestic product — a sum of personal expenditures, investment, government spending and net exports — divided by total labor hours.

You can achieve bounded productivity gains without the macroeconomic relatively easily: consider a manufacturer who adopts technology enabling her to lay off 20% of her workforce — bounded productivity is up but without properly re-absorbing the 20% cut in alternate employment (thereby indirectly adversely affects personal expenditure) or selling more product, there's potential of no or negative macroeconomic productivity growth.

Look at statistics in agriculture, manufacturing and other sectors and what you see are steep bounded labor productivity gains — more output with greater capital and less labor — resulting in a lower share of GDP.

The disconnect between the two productivities, therefore, reflects the process to redeploy or re-value resources — labor, capital, time — to generate GDP growth. Alternately, that lag is reflected by Hal Varian, Chief Economist at Google, "as we adopt technologies that save time ..., that frees up time for market-based activities which will show up in GDP."[3]

---

[3] "Silicon Valley Doesn't Believe U.S. Productivity Is Down", Wall Street Journal.

The key are those market-based activities.

The focus on and excitement about information technology as an investment is understandable: it's nearly everywhere; it scales exponentially; and the variations, opportunity and value to connect disparate points of data, process them through some algorithm and deliver it in real time in a usable form is massive.

The optimism from Silicon Valley — pointing to functionality of the omnipresent smartphone, scalability of applications and the benefits derived from the network of connected people, things and data — sees macroeconomic productivity gains as inevitable and just around the corner.

Completely understandable. But it puts undo faith into things just happening.

I, respectfully, disagree. We need to better understand where we are and agree what needs to happen to craft an approach.

Practically speaking, innovation — an intuitively good thing — does not simply appear in the GDP statistics. A newer automobile may break down less, but that value doesn't appear in the numbers. And, unless consumers or businesses pay for it, it won't. Facebook, Waze and a number of very satisfying and valuable tools benefit users but, again, unless consumers or businesses pay for it, the value won't benefit the numbers either.

Tech and innovation remain hugely important. And getting true bounded productivity improvement from firms through culture, processes, resources and decisions is important from a global competitiveness point of view and is no easy accomplishment.

But the federal government should deliberately shine the spotlight on needed areas of emphasis — specifically both increasing productivity in the service sector and laying out new economic frontiers and markets. Both are needed: the former to up the wages of service workers and the latter to create new markets for growth.

Increasing Productivity in the Service Sector

Employment has been shifting to low productivity sectors over the last 30 years — notably accommodation & food services and healthcare – and it begs the question about how to increase productivity in those sectors either in improving effectiveness (ie., bounded productivity gains) using technology or in improving top line value through the human touch as luxury or experience-enhancement.

In the former instance, as an example consider what Amazon has done to retail and driving the whole omni-channel shopping model as a touchstone and consider where we stand in terms of efficiency in healthcare or education.

In the latter — human touch as luxury or experience enhancement — consider what Starbucks or Nordstrom have done in their respective sectors, using the human touch both in the immediate experience at the retail outlet but also the curation / filter aspect to create an enhanced or luxury experience for the consumer. How do these play out in retail financial services, healthcare or others?[4]

---

[4] Note, as an aside, fundamental difference between pattern-recognizing and extending algorithms – generally self-reinforcing- and the innovation/surprise based dopamine inducing aspect of human taste / fashion.

Finally consider the impact of (unfortunately-named) Baumol's cost disease, which essentially pointed to the fact that (a) there are some tasks that simply cannot be made more efficient — for example a quartet playing a specific Mozart number or a barber cutting hair and (b) in those industries — which will have inherently low productivity growth — real wages will rise faster than inflation. There will be sectors where automation simply isn't plausible and re-valuation of labor will play out.

The federal government, as an employer, plays its own operational part in improving productivity — a point to which I will return — but should otherwise acknowledge the evolving service-based marketplace, what that means in terms of opportunities, wages and employment, and work with employers and sectors to induce investment to improve macroeconomic productivity.

Figure 1. Shift Towards Service Sectors

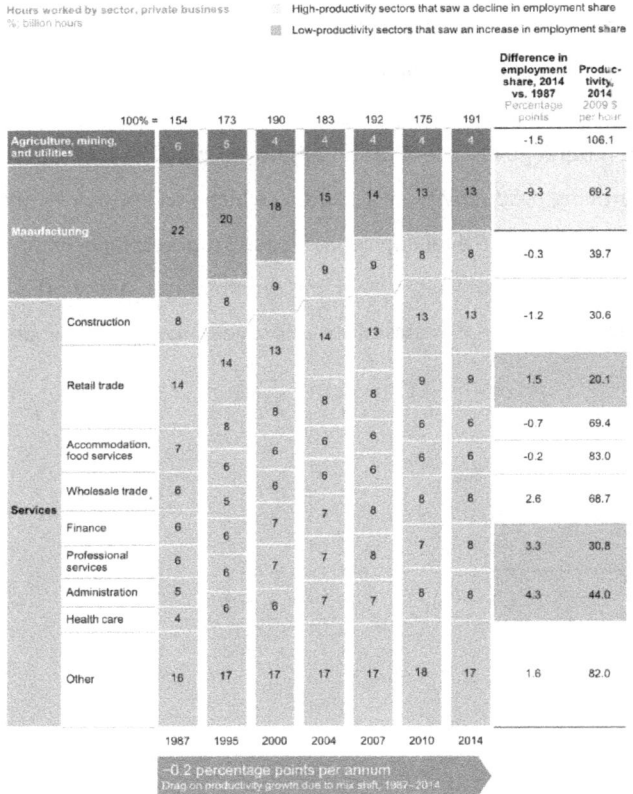

Hours worked by sector, private business
%, billion hours

High-productivity sectors that saw a decline in employment share

Low-productivity sectors that saw an increase in employment share

		100% =	154	173	190	183	192	175	191	Difference in employment share, 2014 vs. 1987 Percentage points	Productivity, 2014 2009 $ per hour
Agriculture, mining, and utilities			6	6	4	4	4	4	4	-1.5	106.1
Manufacturing			22	20	18	15	14	13	13	-9.3	69.2
					9	9	9	8	8	-0.3	39.7
	Construction		8	8				13	13	-1.2	30.6
					13	14	13				
	Retail trade		14	14				9	9	1.5	20.1
					8	8	8				
	Accommodation, food services		7	8	6	6	6	6	6	-0.7	69.4
				6	6	6	6	6	6	-0.2	83.0
	Wholesale trade		6	5	6			8	8	2.6	68.7
Services	Finance		6	6	7	7	8				
	Professional services		6	6	7	7	8	7	8	3.3	30.8
	Administration		5	6	6	7	7	8	8	4.3	44.0
	Health care		4								
	Other		16	17	17	17	17	18	17	1.6	82.0
			1987	1995	2000	2004	2007	2010	2014		

−0.2 percentage points per annum
Drag on productivity growth due to mix shift, 1987–2014

NOTE: Numbers may not sum due to rounding. Based on BLS measures for the private business sector with data only available through 2014.

SOURCE: BLS Multifactor Productivity data; McKinsey Global Institute analysis

Economic frontiers

The other major push should be explicitly re-embracing the spirit of exploring the frontiers of our planet, our human scale and even our reality — with the focus of driving new markets:

- Firmly plant feet off-planet - meaning our Moon, Mars and asteroids. Needless to say this involves a wealth of innovation in energy, engineering, and psychological / behavioral sciences.
- Extend our scale of understanding beyond our human scale, meaning: nano- and quantum engineering at the unit and systems levels within biology, chemistry, computing and manufacturing and meta-engineering at the geologic / planetary scales and beyond.
- Extend our understanding of reality (virtual and augmented) and what it means to be human in a realm where we freely interact with artificial intelligence (and intelligent assistants) and potentially reverse aging.

Extending these frontiers through highlighting the potential and pointing to work already underway speaks to growth, opportunity and creates significant externalities.

You'll note the broad portfolio of sectors inherent within and across the frontiers, and that is intentional. A key part of the initiative is to spur cross-sector industry activity with specific objectives. Why? McKinsey analysis of recent productivity boosts correlated with a broader number of rapid growth sectors.

> During the boom, the number of accelerating sectors for many years was above 20 out of 60 sectors analyzed, in some years making up as much as 30

to 40 percent of total hours worked. In 1995, for example, these included sectors such as retail trade, wholesale trade, finance, and computer and electronic products. Recently only six sectors recorded significant productivity growth acceleration, and those sectors made up only 2 to 7 percent of total hours worked, and 5 to 8 percent of value added. These sectors included oil and gas extraction, petroleum and coal manufacturing, and transportation.[5]

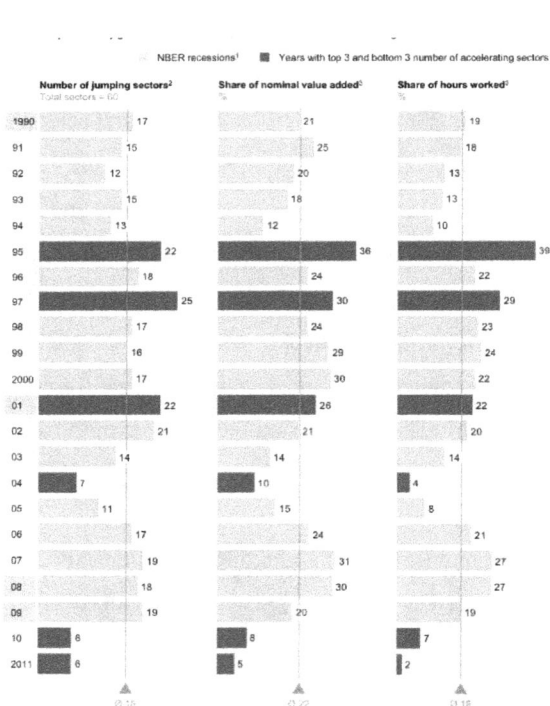

	Number of jumping sectors[2] Total sectors = 60	Share of nominal value added[2] %	Share of hours worked[2] %
1990	17	21	19
91	16	25	18
92	12	20	13
93	15	18	13
94	13	12	10
95	22	36	39
96	18	24	22
97	25	30	29
98	17	24	23
99	16	29	24
2000	17	30	22
01	22	26	22
02	21	21	20
03	14	14	14
04	7	10	4
05	11	15	8
06	17	24	21
07	19	31	27
08	18	30	27
09	19	20	19
10	6	8	7
2011	6	5	2

NBER recessions[1]   ■ Years with top 3 and bottom 3 number of accelerating sectors

1 Indicates years for which a recession covers at least six months of the year.
2 A sector is classified as "accelerating" in year Y if its compound annual growth rate of productivity for years Y through Y + 3 is at least 3 percentage points higher than it was for years Y - 3 to Y.
3 Based on share in Year Y.
NOTE: Based on BLS measures for the private business sector. Data is only available through 2014, therefore last year shown is 2011.

SOURCE: BLS, McKinsey Global Institute analysis

5
https://www.mckinsey.com/~/media/mckinsey/global%20themes/employment%20and%20growth/new%20insights%20into%20the%20slowdown%20in%20us%20productivity%20growth/mgi-the-productivity-puzzle-discussion-paper.ashx

The emphasis here is there are multiple paths needed towards a prosperous economic future, but it starts with acknowledging where we are and why, knowing what levers to pull and setting specific objectives to monitor.

Supporting high value-added, world-leading, enterprises implies we compete globally

Economic power is largely about sitting in the nexus of exchange and knowing how to create value.

We want the US to play in the decision on whether, who and where to hire. This directly implies we want businesses capable of serving the global market of consumers, leveraging the global market of services and competing globally. We also want businesses to focus on high value segments such as R&D-innovation and integration-brand-marketing (rather than exclusively manufacturing-production).

Firms operate on a global landscape — not just overseas competitors pitching to US-based customers and US firms for overseas customers but also in capital, resources, and operations / supply chain — and we want those businesses to want a production or creation footprint here.

And it's not just your known cast of multi-national characters. Couple a high trafficked web front-end like Amazon or Facebook with a social media presence and an efficient and effective supply chain, and a tool box manufacturer in India can easily deliver to a consumer in Indiana or a jeans manufacturer in Los Angeles can reach a consumer in Berlin.

In speaking to these opportunities, it is important to consider economic value-add. Back in 1992, Acer's founder Stan Shih observed "the two ends of the value chain – conception and marketing – command higher values added to the product than the middle part of the value chain – manufacturing" — what's called the Smiling Curve. More recent examples further underscore this point of view.

> In a 2010 study, the Asian Development Bank Institute pulled apart an iPhone and figured that the process of assembling it in China accounted for 3.6 percent of its production cost. The remaining 96.4 percent was paid to the parts suppliers, and Apple, as the creator, claimed the big profits. Net income at Apple, which does almost no manufacturing, was an impressive 21 percent of revenue in its last fiscal year, and its shares trade at 18 times earnings. Meanwhile, Taiwan's Hon Hai Precision Industry Co., one of the companies to which Apple outsources its manufacturing, recorded net profit of 3.5 percent of sales; investors value its shares at 12 times earnings.[6]

This is not to say that manufacturing does not provide good jobs — particularly if productive and supported with capital and innovation — but the economic value creation — and in particular how it ties to wages — is not as simple as Made in the USA.

Understanding the global nature of markets, supply chain and resources and where / how, along the supply chain that value is created, is essential. And applying that understanding in speaking to policy – whether education, trade, etc., is needed.

---

[6] https://www.bloomberg.com/news/articles/2017-06-08/factories-won-t-bring-back-the-american-dream

Note this is by no means a static story either - further complicating matters is the role of artificial intelligence (or intelligent assistance) and 3D printing and how both will potentially continue to affect how value is created.

Use markets and competition to drive dynamism and representative capitalism

With all the talk about disruption, it's ironic that markets have consolidated control to more established, older, firms. And, as previously noted, established firms, on net, cut jobs.

How to drive representative capitalism through regulatory policy? Indirectly but bluntly.

- Remove red tape and occupational-licensing programs that deter new entrants and put undue burden on small business.
- Loosen intellectual property rights — with the specific purpose of reducing barriers to entry inducing new entrants.
- Leverage a rule of thumb for internet transaction data lower competitive barriers to entry — if a platform (e.g., say Facebook) tracks but does not specifically compensate customers for the transaction data implicitly provided to that platform, that data (scrubbed) must be made available to third parties in a well-publicized format and place.[7]
- Introduce a more intuitive antitrust approach that tackles the concentration of data / transactions into a narrow set of players and

---

[7] Note while we are talking about personal data it is also worth reviewing the Third Party doctrine – grounded in 1967 case Katz v United States - setting the precedence that folks who voluntarily provide their information to third parties should have no reasonable expectation of privacy. This simply is not practical in our current environment.

the ability for the incumbent to stay ahead leveraging its capital advantage and rapid replication of innovations by entrants.

- Scrutinize corporate lobbying from the point of view of it as a means of incumbents to protect themselves and be diligent about regulatory or legislative capture – meaning the extent to which those being regulated can set or unduly influence policy to improve their profitability or operating environment.
- Encourage lending and investment platforms and push financial institutions and institutional investors to fund smaller scale firms.

Leverage the opportunities created by the incumbents: operating platforms created by corporate behemoths such as Walmart potentially create fertile environments for new entities to deliver innovative and personalized offerings and also create opportunities given the challenges inherent in giants scaling down with human touch to curate or filter.

This is a fine line and a difficult line to tread, but it points to looking for leadership in the regulatory agencies originating from, notably, emerging companies within the sector.

Establish a central database – accessible to consumers and businesses – to capture and distribute data regarding firms' social impact

Very consistent with representative capitalism, the federal and local governments should aggregate and publish firm-specific scorecards to indicate for example, how much is paid in federal and local taxes, charity contributions, number employed, gender / racial diversity, amount invested in retraining and apprenticeship programs, etc. Even, perhaps, link it with the Better Business

Bureau and social media technologies. And leave it to the consumer or stakeholders to decide on how to act.

Signal and implement structural changes to the healthcare market

To say that healthcare needs an overhaul is not news.

- Healthcare is a huge portion of our economy with costs rising steeply and the potential to crowd-out other spending. Summarized tightly in their "Bending the Curve" report, the Heritage Foundation sums it up well.

  > On a per capita basis, health care spending increased by a factor of six between 1965 and 2005, after adjusting for inflation. In 2008 ... total health care spending in the United States was $2.34 trillion (16.2 percent of GDP), up 4.4 percent from the $2.24 trillion spent the previous year. [8] By contrast, in 1960, total health spending accounted for only 5.2 percent of GDP. Since then, health spending has more than tripled as a percentage of GDP.[9] The Congressional Budget Office (CBO) forecasts that, if present trends continue, health care spending will account for 25 percent of GDP by 2025, 37 percent by 2050, and 49 percent by 2082.[10]

---

[8] Congressional Budget Office, "The Long-Term Outlook for Health Care Spending," November 2007, at http://www.cbo.gov/ftpdocs/87xx/doc8758 /11-13-LT-Health.pdf (February 3, 2010)

[9] Centers for Medicare and Medicaid Services, Office of the Actuary, "National Health Expenditures Web Tables," at http://www.cms.hhs.gov/ NationalHealthExpendData/downloads/tables.pdf (February 3, 2010).

- Rising expense is not necessarily a problem if there are results — but they've not been good either. Studies such the below rank the United States at the bottom of major western industrialized countries on healthcare quality.[11]

	AUS	CAN	FRA	GER	NETH	NZ	NOR	SWE	SWIZ	UK	US
OVERALL RANKING (2013)	4	10	9	5	5	7	7	3	2	1	11
Quality Care	2	9	8	7	5	4	11	10	3	1	5
Effective Care	4	7	9	6	5	2	11	10	8	1	3
Safe Care	3	10	2	6	7	9	11	5	4	1	7
Coordinated Care	4	8	9	10	5	2	7	11	3	1	6
Patient-Centered Care	5	8	10	7	3	6	11	9	2	1	4
Access	8	9	11	2	4	7	6	4	2	1	9
Cost-Related Problem	9	5	10	4	8	6	3	1	7	1	11
Timeliness of Care	6	11	10	4	2	7	8	9	1	3	5
Efficiency	4	10	8	9	7	3	4	2	6	1	11
Equity	5	9	7	4	8	10	6	1	2	2	11
Healthy Lives	4	8	1	7	5	9	6	2	3	10	11
Health Expenditures/Capita, 2011*	$3,800	$4,522	$4,118	$4,495	$5,099	$3,182	$5,669	$3,925	$5,643	$3,405	$8,508

Notes: * Includes ties. ** Expenditures shown in $US PPP (purchasing power parity); Australian $ data are from 2010.
Source: Calculated by The Commonwealth Fund based on 2011 International Health Policy Survey of Sicker Adults; 2012 International Health Policy Survey of Primary Care Physicians; 2013 International Health Policy Survey; Commonwealth Fund National Scorecard 2011; World Health Organization; and Organization for Economic Cooperation and Development, OECD Health Data, 2013 (Paris: OECD, Nov. 2013).

- Finally, life expectancy also varies by as much as 20 years across counties in the US.[12]

---

[10] Congressional Budget Office, "The Long-Term Outlook for Health Care Spending."

[11] https://www.washingtonpost.com/news/to-your-health/wp/2014/06/16/once-again-u-s-has-most-expensive-least-effective-health-care-system-in-survey/?utm_term=.c2a8906858b5

[12] https://www.washingtonpost.com/news/to-your-health/wp/2017/05/08/u-s-life-expectancy-varies-by-more-than-20-years-from-county-to-county/?utm_term=.a5130446d14f

Recent debates have been grounded in select principles: healthcare as a universal right (attributed to the left), decreasing expenses through turning down federal government funding (attributed to the right), or concerns over an over-interventionist government (also attributed to the right).

Principles matter — in fact I would argue all of the above are valid — but our healthcare problem is a structural one demanding focus on operational details, not sound-bites. Not the stuff of exciting headlines. But important. And the layer at which we need to operate to get things done.

To get beyond talk and get results, the federal government needs to lead a coordinated effort with states and industry. Core principles of Healthcare 2.0:

- People should be able to choose level of coverage.[13]
- People should have some baseline / minimum access to healthcare and insurance.[14]
- People should benefit from positive choices and bear the cost of bad choices.
- The system should effectively apply market mechanisms in innovation, consumption, capital investment, etc. while also acknowledging that healthcare is a different kind of good and not like simply buying a shirt.
- The system should align behaviors and incentives of providers and consumers around care, quality and delivery.

[13] Be mindful, the context is in the US.

[14] Health insurance - assuming affordable - seems the 'right' thing to do - otherwise the burden falls on family or society.

- The system should be engineered to equalize the genetic lottery.

What I believe Healthcare 2.0 looks like (and keeping it relatively simple here):

- On the payer side, insurance should be directly with individuals (not through place of employment) and orient towards a fee for care model rather than fee for service with a baseline set of services, ability to choose options and exposure / visibility to costs.[15]
- Medicaid should remain a safety net to subsidize low income Americans.
- Insurance industry needs to scale in a way that pools risk but maintains close touch with the consumer. That touch can be developed / enhanced through technology (wearables to communicate activity, pay transactions with grocery stores regarding purchases).

---

[15] Per the CBO - *the percentage of health care spending paid "out of pocket" by patients has fallen substantially, from 52% in 1965 to only 15% in 2005 — meaning that third-party payments have increased from 48% to 85%. As the proportion of third-party payer has increased, total spending has grown even faster. Since 1965, real per capita health care expenditures have increased approximately six-fold.

Factor in an oft-cited RAND study that randomly placed participants in various insurance programs where the free-health-care group spent 45% more health care per person than the highest-spending cost-sharing group and predictably, while spending decreased as the cost borne by the consumer increased, the biggest jump was from the free-care plan to the lowest cost-sharing plan.

From these results, many analysts have concluded that free health care and insurance with lower cost sharing has little substantial effect on health but contributes significantly to higher health care spending.

- Use reinsurance — effectively insurance for insurance companies to transfer components of their risk portfolio — to offset the more significant risks across pools.

- Standardized, scrubbed and available datasets covering a broad population set must be publicly available, including a broad range of variables (genetics, activity — physical and mental, intake — physical and mental) over time to be leveraged in R&D through to assessment.

- Deliver healthcare services through more cost-effective channels. Hospitals are the most expensive platform to deliver — so reduce dependency on them where possible — and increase prevalence of nurses, pharmacists, and other non-physician health professionals delivering clinical services for which they are trained and capable. Use telemedicine to improve efficiencies and effectiveness.

- Regulatory scrutiny on outcomes, cost effectiveness, and intellectual property. On service delivery, assess relative costs and outcomes across geography. On healthcare suppliers / big pharma, lean towards decisions to deflate expenses (simplify / shorten approval process, shortening IP windows, introducing generics).

Establish a Healthcare 2.0 Task Force (H2TF) with a three-prong platform: Tech, Industry Reach-Out, Analysis & Recommendation

The Tech prong should work with industry leaders to develop (a) standard tagged datasets that can be used all across the industry (b) set the process to capture user health information and guidelines for validating / scrubbing the data to ensure accuracy and privacy and (c) setting up and monitoring the data warehouse.

Industry Reach-Out prong is about working with states and industry to shape the set-up - particularly on the payer side (e.g., hospital billing, insurance, etc.). Again, more activist than I prefer but important to move things forward.

Analysis & Recommendation is about reporting on key metrics and pushing data points to action. For example:

- Focusing on the potential critical impact of obesity (Body Mass Index > 30) as the potential underlying cause of top 15 conditions and disproportionate spending.
- A Kaiser Family Foundation "analysis shows that the 1% of the population with the highest spending accounted for almost one quarter of health spending (21%) and that the top 5% of the population is responsible for almost half of all spending"[16]
- Inter-region differences also suggest action. An increase may not necessarily mean waste if the investment generates positive outcomes but, if there's no measurable difference - which some studies have shown - then differences should raise a question.

   ... the case of a hypothetical 75-year-old male presenting with new onset chest pain with exertion, approximately the same percentage of doctors in both high-spending and low-spending regions recommended a stress test, but doctors in high-spending regions were much more likely to order an echocardiogram, refer to a cardiologist, or admit the patient to a hospital. Presented with a case of an exacerbation of end-stage congestive heart failure, doctors in high-spending regions were more likely to admit the patient to an acute medicine floor or an intensive care unit (ICU).

---

[16] https://www.kff.org/slideshow/how-health-expenditures-vary-across-the-population-slideshow/

For 100 patients of each clinical vignette, doctors in the highest-quintile spending region recommended an average of 80 more hypertension follow-up visits annually, 14 more spiral CTs, 25 more echocardiograms, 24 more coronary care unit admissions, and 29 more GI referrals than doctors in the lowest-quintile spending region recommended. The authors concluded that doctors in high-spending and low-spending regions were equally likely to recommend therapeutic and diagnostic interventions strongly supported by the literature, but doctors in higher-spending regions tended to recommend less-well-supported services at a much higher frequency.[17]

Set the budgetary expectations

Healthcare 2.0 may take several years to get on-track — but signal now. Being clear that the expectation is to see the bend in four to five years based on the trajectory is important to guide decisions and actions of participants.

Regulators should bias towards using markets and competition to drive innovation

I noted this point more generally before, but it deserves further mention. Dynamics in the healthcare market have prevented technology and commoditization from generating deflationary pressures in healthcare sector seen elsewhere.

That must change.

---

[17] Brenda Sirovich, Patricia M. Gallagher, David E. Wennberg, and Elliott S. Fisher, "Discretionary Decision Making by Primary Care Physicians and the Cost of U.S. Health Care," Health Affairs, Vol. 27, No. 3 (May/June 2008), pp. 813-823,
at http://content.healthaffairs.org/cgi/reprint/27/3/813 (May 24, 2009).

This is not about casting stones at any of the market participants. There are certainly some high profile egregious acts, but it is in the natural and appropriate interest of pharma to extend IP protection and prevent entry of generics as it is in the interest of healthcare suppliers to work within the rules of the system to maximize profits.

Our structural issues in healthcare — high prices, sub-par results on average — necessitate assertive, constructive action to move the market in the appropriate direction. Healthcare is a long-term play, and we need to start making moves now.

Leverage Unemployment Insurance to support a work force and local economies buffeted by disruption

Unemployment Insurance (UI) provides the means to financially buffer individuals and families in the case of a layoff, expedite reemployment and flex, when needed, given economic downturns.

Much of the current UI program is good but the recipiency rate (percentage of unemployed getting benefits) remains well down from recent historical run-rates of about 38% to currently below 28% — suggesting aspects of eligibility ought to be reviewed — and there is significant variation among the states that ought to be addressed.

Many of the specifics and execution lies — and should lie — at the state level, but the federal government should take several steps.

At the most basic level:

- Set minimum standards for benefits. benefits should be a minimum of half and up to two thirds of state average weekly earnings and a basic minimum duration of 26 weeks.
- Reset the minimum taxable wage base, index it to inflation, and set the net federal tax rate to offset too steep an increase. The current taxable wage base is $7000, had not been changed since 1983 (it should be closer to $40k if indexed).
- Standardize the Extended Benefits model — which kicks-in and extends UI benefits when unemployment is high — usually adding 13 weeks (but some states potentially another 7 if unemployment is very high).

Modernizing UI to both the changing nature of work and the workforce and factoring disruption created by trade and technology is also critical:

- Adjust baseline eligibility requirements: set base period to four financial quarters prior to job loss; use hours rather than earnings to bring low and moderate wage earners in; enable reentrants into the work force to apply if they would have been eligible prior to a leave (e.g., caring for a parent or child); allow the work test to include part-time work while searching for a new job; allow for disruption events (e.g., potentially a primary earner's job moves and the spouse is forced to leave their job in the move).
- Encourage experimentation of wage insurance within the UI framework. Research[18] points to a net drop in pay of approximately

---

[18] http://conference.iza.org/conference_files/ESSLE2009/wachter_t964.pdf

From Till Von Wachter, Jae Song, and Joyce Manchester, "Long-Term Earnings Losses Due to Mass Layoffs during the 1982 Recession: An Analysis Using Longitudinal Administrative Data from 1974 to 2008," working paper,

$15k per annum in salary following a layoff and highlights that workers in their 20s and 30s have historically recovered their earnings better than those in their 40s and older. President Obama proposed a program of up to $10k over two years — effectively a third — up to $50k.

- Enable self-employed individuals — one could extend this notion eventually to address eligibility gaps and consider how to roll wage insurance in potentially as well for broader constituencies — to contribute to private unemployment accounts.

Finally, it's important to keep a foot in the work door for a few reasons. In that light:

- UI eligibility should support part-time work during job search
- The federal government should push re-training and apprenticeship programs — emphasize cooperation between education and business to enhance training and preparedness through micro-degrees and training programs.
- Encourage experimentation with short-term compensation (STC). The idea of the program is to allow workers to draw pro-rated UI benefits while working a limited number of hours as an alternative to a layoff. There are obvious risks to manipulate the system, but if it encourages folks to continue working — and encourages companies to keep folks on the books — value proposition seems common sense.

Again, minor adjustments to UI in general but important to modernize.

University of California-Los Angeles (2011)

Prudent immigration policy grounded on economics

The United States was built with immigrants. And I understand the emotional and principled arguments well[19].

As in healthcare, the discussions have been sourced in broad principles and if we instead step away from the emotion and take a more granular look at specific questions and issues, points of general agreement[20] take shape:

- A March 2017 CNN/ORC poll found that 71% do not believe in deporting all undocumented immigrants, while 78% favor deporting criminal immigrants.
- The same March 2017 CNN/ORC poll found a strong majority of Americans, 90%, approve of a pathway to citizenship so long as immigrants fulfill requirements like having been here for a number of years, holding a job, speaking English, and are willing to pay back taxes that they owe.
- A June 2017 Gallup poll pointed out 72%of respondents say immigrants take jobs Americans don't want. As previously documented, that includes workers in the agricultural and food processing industries.
- According to a Politico/Morning Consult poll, two-thirds of respondents supported allowing more college educated or highly skilled immigrants into the country (vs less than 50% for low skilled) and respondents were split on whether to increase or decrease H1-Bs.

Demographically, immigration has both grown the population and held the median age down - both aspects having important macro-economic impacts.

---

[19] Also, as disclosure, I am the son of immigrants and the first American born in my family.
[20] I am taking the liberty of defining general agreement as greater than two-thirds.

According to Pew: "(i)f no immigrants had entered the country after 1965 ... the nation's population still would have grown—to 252 million people by 2015, rather than 324 million. The population would have grown by less than half as much as it actually did (30% vs. 67% growth)." From a distribution point of view, immigration also has resulted in younger population — in 2015 without immigration, median age would have been 41 as opposed to 38[21] — playing out favorably in healthcare and economics dynamics.

The aforementioned frames immigration reform practically:

- Pathway to citizenship should be available for law-abiding dreamers and migrants already in the country.
- Emphasis on merit-based view rather than family-based approach for accepting legal immigration — although, over time, could scale that up if appropriate.

Reciprocity & hospitality

If a visitor knocks on your door in the dead of a cold winter's night, what should you do? What should they do?

Immigration often focuses on the obligations of the host — fair given the relative positions of power.

But the visitor — viewed through the lens of reciprocity — has obligations too: help out and follow fair and reasonable house rules. So if, for example, the host family removes their shoes upon entry to keep the dirt out, that seems appropriate for guests to follow also.

---

[21] http://www.pewhispanic.org/2015/09/28/chapter-2-immigrations-impact-on-past-and-future-u-s-population-change/

A good host should go out of their way to make a guest feel comfortable, but the extent of their obligation is a question and a matter of choice.

The common-sense trade-off regarding the responsibilities of host and guest under principle of reciprocity should apply more generally with immigration.

Invest in priority infrastructure addressing the prior points

Infrastructure deservedly receives much airtime as an opportunity given the current state of our systems that transports, stores and supports the movement of people, resources, data and services. The American Society of Civil Engineers' 2017 report maintained the D+ overall rating and estimated current funding gap of about $2 trillion between now and 2025. There are other statistics that paint a decidedly less grim picture but there's little doubt investment is needed.

As in the case of Healthcare 2.0, Infrastructure incorporates specific areas of focus and adjustments in policy to encourage / speed investment as well as manage expenses and stretch federal dollars.

Areas of focus should target those areas directly impacting dynamism, namely broadband access to support remote training and employment notably in rural communities impacted by disruption, and surface and air transport enabling longer distance commuting (thereby allowing individuals access to more jobs and employers greater access to candidates).

On the policy front, the federal government should:

- Continue the practice of a coordinating high profile / focus projects across federal departments.

- Narrow the NEPA (National Environment Protection Act) needs for the focus projects in particular (while continuing to look at how to modernize NEPA in common sense fashion, such as considering major environmental issues and incorporating previous analyses of similar projects).

- Reverse Executive Order 13502, which required use of Project Labor Agreements for federally funded projects – effectively requiring contractors to sign collective bargaining agreements with construction unions before the project.

- Temporarily suspend the Davis-Bacon Act for focus areas and review the method of calculating the prevailing wage used therein. While the concept of the Davis-Bacon Act makes sense to ensure that the federal government pays a reasonable wage for work performed, the calculation of the prevailing wage according to studies sets it at 22 percent greater than market rate thereby increasing inefficiencies.[22]

- Focus on long-term capability – structurally – through (a) partnerships with local governments and private entities, (b) standardizing the application process across regions, (c) developing a database to enable better information regarding current and past projects / evaluations to support bench-marking and transparency.[23]

---

[22] http://www.beaconhill.org/BHIStudies/PrevWage08/DavisBaconPrevWage080207Final.pdf

[23] This reflects the operating philosophy of federal government as a portfolio enterprise – a subject to which I will return later

Digression – Reciprocity & Actuality

Reciprocity and actuality are core to the pragmatic principles because both reflect who we, as Americans, want to be, idealistically and practically, given they facilitate interactions across heterogeneous environments.

In his recent book "Ordinary Virtues", Michael Ignatieff travelled to various global points where there is a significant amount of local, immediate cross-cultural interaction coupled with some amount of social duress. His objective? To understand how people from varied cultures and belief systems actually interact by looking at active mixing-pot environments: was it some sense of global morality frameworks (e.g, religion or secular grounded views around liberalism) or something else? He concludes that individuals ...

> make up their moral life as they go along, with fewer authorities to guide or coerce them. We never heard anyone argue as if moral choice was a matter of simply following what some priestly or political authority told them to think.... This in turn helps to reinforce the sense in which, when we make choices, we are not obeying time-honored universal commands, but rather thinking through, for ourselves, what our situation demands.... (E)quality of voice and moral choice as an individual responsibility were the two new expectations we observed everywhere.

What we want in interactions with others should not surprise: fairness, justice, tolerance, and hospitality (when warranted). These make up what I am labeling **reciprocity**. (Golden Rule anyone?)

Actuality is about dealing with what is directly in front of us rather than universal principles — explicitly relying less on abstractions or labels and ultimately more on deciding and acting with common sense in the specific context in a way that could hold up to face-to-face scrutiny and discussion.

Both reciprocity and actuality play outsized roles in pragmatism given their practical, effective importance within heterogeneous environments.

Part II — Rebuild Civic Dynamics

The Agenda is founded where law and principles intersect. However, it's not all black & white. Consider the following examples:

- The interplay of the constitutional right to free speech with our societal moral sense of right and wrong with our personal reaction of support or being offended.
- The right of individuals to their privacy and beliefs with society's norms, security and shared outlook.
- How to balance creating opportunity for a specific disadvantaged individual v eliminating an opportunity for an otherwise capable individual.
- How to balance an omnipresent media torrent fed by a number of objectives (including profits, product awareness / branding and/or political messaging) and a relatively concentrated set of commercial gateways with the incredible empowerment of choice that comes with the internet.

There are few clear-cut answers to the questions at the federal level. The federal government plays a part — as representative, legal arbiter and policy maker — but it neither belongs in every debate or discussion nor does it have the legal remit, capability or nuanced knowledge to effectively perform at the local / granular level.

Nor is there necessarily a market through which price signals of supply and demand can be processed and aggregated by an enterprise.

That means we need to rebuild the ability to collectively and constructively talk and work through and among thorny issues — re-establishing 'civic dynamics' — and embrace reciprocity through tolerance, fairness, justice, and hospitality — and it's the role of the federal government to set up and support those dynamics through policy and setting the example.

Let's talk through one of the examples — free speech v societal moral sense of right & wrong v personal reaction — and then generalize.

- Folks and companies have the right to their individual beliefs and choices and the right to express them under the First Amendment. That is non-negotiable[24].
- There is no Amendment stating someone won't be offended by someone else's freedom of expression or will always be agreed with (you have the right to speak your mind and respond under the First Amendment — although a sense of humor, slightly thicker skin and modesty help).
- The media torrent provides a set of channels and platforms through which to communicate and exchange. The editorial perspective of many are known (e.g., Fox, CNN, The New York Times, Sinclair, NPR). The algorithms of the tech entries (Facebook, Twitter notably) — particularly given ad-based revenue — are currently opaque.
- Grass-roots efforts that effectively leverage the media channels can affect change, calling attention to issues and pushing for change directly or pointing out how consumers or businesses can apply

---

[24] Hate speech — defined specifically as speech that poses an imminent risk of unlawful action, where the speaker has the intention to create such action and there is the likelihood that the speech will result in the action — excepted.

leverage (usually economic) to achieve an outcome (note that these efforts are available to all).

- Understand the difference between winning an argument (truly swaying a point of view) v the other side simply no longer arguing — the long-term impacts (or resentment) can be significant.

In this case, the federal government is responsible to:

Uphold the law; emphasize the mores. It's easy and optically expedient to express outrage. Harder to underscore the law. Important, too, to set the example and demonstrate a little stoicism, show how to confront adversity or alternate views, and how to attack problems (what do we know about current state, how the dynamics work and what we want / what do we agree or disagree on / what don't we know).

Ensure competitive factors enable representation of alternate views. Representative capitalism ought be a constant touchstone. In this case, it's considering media outlets.

Demonstrate how to handle disagreements. Where reasonable, use the disagreement to create dialogue. Understand, too, that from a reciprocity point of view, the more powerful one has an obligation to set the tone.

Understand the dynamic specifically in question and identify whether it merits a policy change. In this specific case and with questionable content perpetuated on social media, is there a need to improve transparency of context and messaging — for example imposing old school journalistic standards to distinguish / place paid-for content v member created and self-prioritized v algorithm based.

Likewise, as virtual and augmented realities take shape the question of how to apply rules and ethics — and taking lessons from massive multiplayer online games (MMOs) — absolutely must apply.

This clearly is not the federal government acting in isolation - but it can work with entities to explore, clarify and facilitate the discussion and set common sense guidelines.

Manage change and support to reframe hot-button belief issues to address longer-term resentment.

Here I borrow heavily from "Everybody Lies: Big Data, New Data, and What the Internet Can Tell Us About Who We Really Are" as I think the premise of the book (using Google searches as a means at getting at truth insights) is extraordinarily powerful.

To set the background, the section looks at hate and prejudice by correlating negative words with social groups such as Muslims, Gays and Christians.

> Muslims are the only group stereotyped (meaning high correlation) as terrorists. When a Muslim American plays into this stereotype, the response can be instantaneous and vicious. Google search data can give us a minute-by-minute peek into such eruptions of hate-fueled rage. Consider what happened shortly after the mass shooting in San Bernardino, California, on December 2, 2015. That morning, Rizwan Farook and Tashfeen Malik entered a meeting of Farook's coworkers armed with semiautomatic pistols and semiautomatic rifles and murdered fourteen people.... The top Google search in California with the word "Muslims" in it at the time was "kill Muslims.".... While hate searches were approximately 20 percent of all searches about Muslims before the attack, more than half of all search volume about Muslims became hateful in the hours that followed it....

In (President Obama's speech after the attack) ... the president said, "It is the responsibility of all Americans—of every faith—to reject discrimination." But searches calling Muslims "terrorists," "bad," "violent," and "evil" doubled during and shortly after the speech.... Obama asked Americans to "not forget that freedom is more powerful than fear." Yet searches for "kill Muslims" tripled during his speech....

Two months after that original speech, Obama gave another televised speech on Islamophobia, this time at a mosque.... Obama spent little time insisting on the value of tolerance. Instead, he focused overwhelmingly on provoking people's curiosity and changing their perceptions of Muslim Americans. Many of the slaves from Africa were Muslim, Obama told us; Thomas Jefferson and John Adams had their own copies of the Koran; the first mosque on U.S. soil was in North Dakota; a Muslim American designed skyscrapers in Chicago. Obama again spoke of Muslim athletes and armed service members but also talked of Muslim police officers and firefighters, teachers and doctors. And my analysis of the Google searches suggests this speech was more successful than the previous one. Many of the hateful, rageful searches against Muslims dropped in the hours after the president's address.

The lesson: if folks hold a belief, they will continue holding it if you go at it directly — even if presented with what you think is data or a cogent argument.

Approached indirectly through engaging curiosity or appealing to another direction can be more effective in achieving outcomes. Takes more time and creativity, but better results.

Modernize rights in the face of technology change. Understand that the virtual / data world is here to stay and now having some experience with it, it seems time to take stock of what it means for our Rights.

Data privacy and the third-party doctrine is an obvious case but less obvious may be rules regarding sexual harassment in augmented and virtual realities, rights of individuals to control or profit from their digital trail, or rights of disadvantaged genotypes.

This should be an area defined by legislation rather than through the courts.

Digression – Power through Flow (vs Walls)

Sustained power is derived from four things - any of which lacking, eventually undermines it:

- **Resources and know-how.** People. Money. Military capability. Assets that create economic value.
- **Organization.** A structure and/or process that enables decisions to be made and lessons to be learned and adopted - effectively and efficiently.
- **Flow.** Resources preserved behind a castle wall may provide a degree of security, but power is dynamic: knowledge to create economic, scientific, or military value; capability to engage, do and sway.
- **Perceived track record of success.** People imbue a perceived winner a sense of competence or authority - confidence that something they're doing is right.

This is an open, confident, engaged and transparent view of power distinct from a fortress view where power is held and withheld to strengthen and secure oneself.

Arguably flow may even have a higher short-term cost than fortress. Building a wall indeed costs money. Investing the time and attention to engage and accommodate the interactions likely costs more. But it is well worth it.

Follow history and you see economic power and growth comes through being at the nexus of interactions. Isolation eventually leads the other direction. Walls may provide some visible assurance in the context of military power and security but, too walled off, there is no real view into — or effect on — what is going on beyond those walls.

From a security POV, flow and organization is not only about economics but, through interactions with neighbors creates relationships, knowledge, and influence. If you hide behind the walls, who knows what the opposition and neighbors are up to?

Part III — Focus Foreign & Defense Policy

The agenda for foreign and defense policy lies at the nexus o our national interests and macro changes in technology, geo-politics and associated knock-on effects.

We need to be clear about what our national interests are and, more importantly, what they are not.

National interest is not defined by moral outrage or emotion. Rather it is where we, for practical reasons, are willing to invest time, resources and attention or, at worst, sacrifice the lives of our women and men for the cause.

Our national interests are, simply:

- Strong and secure nation across such vectors as food & water, energy, financial system, military (defense), infrastructure, migration, social cohesion and intellectual property / know-how.
- Stable and fair international order and commerce. ('Fair' is a slippery and subjective word — but deliberately chosen.)
- Credibility — in the specific sense that we have the prudence & capability to set, communicate and achieve our objectives — and that we keep to our allies and commitments appropriately.

Two key developments of macro changes must be borne in mind: defense and evolving tech.

On the defense, other parties, notably both China and Russia, have had ample opportunity to study the United States' military capabilities and political will —

and adjusted their strategies focusing either on asymmetries, new fronts, or some combination:

- Anti-access / area denial technologies (A2/AD) to take advantage of asymmetric strategic presence and leverage the fact that the United States often projects military force. The objective of of a multi-layered A2/AD is to reduce the ability of the US to bring its forces to bear. China for example may target satellites to impact US military data and communications and an array of land-based air missiles, fast missile boats, and missile submarines to create a buffer zone around its mainland.
- Grey zone tactics to take advantage of asymmetric interests — areas where the United States' interests are fuzzy but there are tactical advantages on their side.
- AI / robotic based swarm and precision technologies that directly offset America's traditional strengths.

For smaller and non-state parties, asymmetry is more in concealment and shielding — again effectively preventing application of full force from the US military by either hiding or dwelling among the population.

Evolving tech — notably currently space and cyber — also change and complicate the game. For example:

- **Space**. Strategically speaking, space is the ultimate High Ground, holds a key set of intelligence and communication assets (satellites) and is potentially a source for resources. Leading a strategic military capability in space is a must.

FORWARD: A PRAGMATIC AGENDA

In August of 2017, China and Russia signed a multi-year agreement to partner on lunar missions, satellites, developing new materials, researching space debris and remote monitoring of Earth. This should spur some concern.

While much is being done in the private sector — with Elon Musk's SpaceX, Richard Branson's Virgin Galactic, and Jeff Bezos's Blue Origin — to increase accessibility to space, more must be done to structurally bring down expenses and apply commercial business practices to bring down NASA's expense. "Stepping Stones: Economic Analysis"[25] study released late in 2017 and commissioned by NASA frames an assertive and potentially effective path forward:

> (U)se of asteroid resources, combined with best commercial business practices, succeeds in reducing the costs by more than a factor of 4 (from about $390B to about $90B) for a robust plan of human exploration of the lunar surface, NEOs (near earth objects such as asteroids), and eventually the surface of Mars. Assuming a reasonable investment by NASA in the initial DDT&E (design, development, test and evaluation) for the elements of this architecture and commitment to use the capability provided at a reasonable price, along with the ability to obtain adequate initial start-up capital, this approach does so in a fashion that can create a self-sustaining business in space resources that achieves an estimated profit of >20% annually before the end of 20 years....

> This business can be further expanded and made even more profitable through development and fielding of more advanced designs of key elements over time. This further reduces the cost of asteroid resources and provides increased commercial support to a

---

[25] https://www.nasa.gov/sites/default/files/atoms/files/eso_final_report.pdf

burgeoning space tourism business and even enables cost effective development of various sized (100s to 1000s of inhabitants) space habitats and the eventual colonization of space.

It is worth noting that the study's authors generate about a quarter to a third of their US$300 billion savings from NASA adopting commercial best practices and the balance using space-based methods of acquiring propellant and material.

- **Cyber**. Pervasive connectivity through networks to hardware, applications and data creates new risks throughout the dimensions that we are only just starting to see.

  Similar to trade — where focus has often been on macro-benefits and less on the structural cracks — pervasive IT brings prominent net benefits as well as risks and concerns that need to be understood. And evolving robotics, nanotech, biotech, additive manufacturing and AI only complicate matters further.

  Important, too, is the notion that technology changes not only complicate the vectors / lines of warfare but also the actors: increased availability and shrinking costs of technology — coupled with global/instant communications and social media — allows coordination and effectiveness of non-state actors — thereby complicating the security picture.

How do national interests and evolving tech overlap to layout the agenda?

Maintain military superiority and defensive strength across the more complex range of warfare (new fronts, risks and actors).

Geopolitical opponents such as China and Russia, and regional threats North Korea have and are investing heavily. We cannot afford falling behind or not adequately addressing the risks.

Continuing to focus on the capability of standard military hard power projection leveraging technology is critical — meaning applying AI, detection / sensing, engineer in multiple environments (air / sea / space / electromagnetic) to enable precise and timely offensive strikes is critical in order to offset developments previously noted.

While we want to be cautious in overly militarizing space, there is urgency and, given the reasons previously mentioned, we cannot fall behind. Delineating a clear strategy and commitment is crucial.

In cyber, China's focus on tech is widespread and well-known. While there are questions to the degree it's centrally controlled or organic / networked, China's capability is deep and impact significant and pervasive. Foreign Policy magazine estimated 50k to 100k socially linked hackers[26] whereas Mandiant tied hacks into 141 organizations across 20 industries back to Unit 61398 — a secret unit of China's military.[27]

Russia's activities leveraging bots and troll army have sought to influence elections in US and France and cyberattacks in Estonia have been well-documented.[28] It's also important to note the distinctively psychologically manipulative flavor — using disinformation and propaganda — in addition to standard cyber means, to achieve strategic objectives.

---

[26] https://foreignpolicy.com/2010/03/03/chinas-hacker-army/
[27] https://www.fireeye.com/blog/threat-research/2013/02/mandiant-exposes-apt1-chinas-cyber-espionage-units.html
[28] https://www.theguardian.com/technology/2017/dec/02/fake-news-botnets-how-russia-weaponised-the-web-cyber-attack-estonia

North Korea's nuclear ballistic ambitions may often have center stage but its army's over 6000 hackers have demonstrated results not only hacking Sony Pictures in 2014, allegedly were behind the WannaCry cyberattack in May 2017, attempted to steal $1B from the New York Federal Reserve and a "former British intelligence chief estimates the take from its cyberheists may bring the North as much as $1 billion a year, or a third of the value of the nation's exports."[29]

The Defense Science Board issued a report in February 2017 on Cyber Deterrence recommending bolstering cyber defenses — notably deterrence campaigns tailored to global state players such as Russia and China, regional state players such as North Korea and Iran and persistent non-state actors, developing a cyber-threat resilient 'thin line' for key US assets (e.g., infrastructure), and enhance general foundational capabilities.[30]

However, it is not just about the military. Some steps regarding cyber and national security may simply be policy — for example, as I noted previously, applying old school journalistic mores to social media platforms and clearly distinguish paid-for content from feeds / algorithm pulls from editorialized content to minimize foreign interference.

Two underlying differences of cyber versus traditional military defense are worth keeping in mind: the more a country leverages cyber the more capable it is and the more vulnerable it is to attack (this creates a certain risk asymmetry versus a less generally advanced nation like, say, North Korea); also cyber is an on-going process looking not only at the technology stack and rigorous

---

[29] The New York Times. "The World Once Laughed at North Korea Cyberpower. No More." October 16 2017
[30] https://www.acq.osd.mil/dsb/reports/2010s/DSB-CyberDeterrenceReport_02-28-17_Final.pdf

identification / communication of vulnerabilities but also the social and process hacks that can circumvent technical protection.

Focus on our own A2/AD capability — at scale and range

Our overseas interests — like formal, signed, alliances such as NATO and key trade lanes such as the Suez Canal, Panama Canal, and the South China Sea — must remain secure. And in achieving that, our military strength and the ability to project hard power is crucial.

Also, however, is the ability to project A2/AD 'hard nets' — here using the term to cover protective shields (preventing, for example, missiles from coming in) as well as containment (preventing missiles from coming out). The former need is straight-forward but the latter increasingly relevant to isolate regimes that choose not to abide by international standards — with the intent to remove their threat to others.

The current primary architecture are the missile defense systems including the Patriot, Terminal High Altitude Area Defense (THAAD) ballistic missile defense system, Aegis (including Ashore) and the supporting Army/Navy Transportable Radar (AN/TPY-2) that provides the supporting surveillance capability. All of these missile systems are kinetic in that they do not carry warheads and fundamentally work by physically intercepting the projectile.

Development on this front must aggressively continue.

While the systems have largely been successful in specific contexts (Patriot for point protection and THAAD for short and mid-range) both can be swamped, and neither are currently effective against long-range missiles such as ICBMs (although the supporting radar systems can provide surveillance/ acquisition).

Lockheed Martin — the manufacturers of THAAD — is developing THAAD-ER which purportedly will extend the range of THAAD, provide it potentially loitering / adjustment capability, and travel at higher speeds.

But this is an area we need to continue to press on to cope with greater quantities, ballistic innovations — physical, electromagnetic, and informational.

Soft power for long term influence.

The most strategic of all.

Our nation's heterogeneous environment equips us to exert influence in a world mindful of long term security threats while recognizing the importance of self-determination.

Here the objectives are both (a) to engage the levers that create and weaponize isolation and disassociation into radicalization and (b) where appropriate, address the information asymmetries enabling concealment.

In the former case:

- Invest in and be ever mindful of Brand USA. It is important that the US is seen as strong, energetic and successful and, in total, good citizens to ourselves and the world. Do our best to live up to our principles.

- Influence is not just about nation-states. Formal law is written by states but many of the thorny issues we're dealing with are about groups as defined by beliefs, culture and history. While we cannot address every perceived issue and it's not our role to pry into others' domestic affairs, it's in our long-run interest (and in theirs) to support discussions that enhance representativeness of outliers.

- Consider a Fairness Doctrine. 'Fairness' as a concept is deeply hard-wired — consider studies with capuchins (and replicated with other animals) demonstrating their reaction to unfair pay / treatment (the one receiving cucumber and having performed the requisite task, hurls the cucumber back after seeing its mate receive a grape — perceived as a greater reward — for the same task) or consider too that nearly every significant world belief system has something like reciprocity baked-in.

  Exactly what fair means will vary culture to culture, between people and may change over time.

  But certain questions should be considered, like how secure is the second party or alternate views or how is the representation or integration of social groups in political, economic, or financial systems?

The latter case presents a difficult balancing act: US national security interests v perception of fairness and risk of creating radicalization if the US is perceived to be using its military might inappropriately.

The objective of a soft power strategy is to shape influence and support the development of representative leaders and institutions while establishing relationships and accumulating potentially valuable information — notably in more volatile areas.

Part IV — Address Structural Flaws in Government

Like any organization facing dynamic conditions, the federal government's role needs to be defined, periodically refined, and obligated to perform effectively and efficiently.

Government however is not a business — it is distinct in that it sets the rules (and also polices and judges same) so we therefore need to structurally guard against self-interests of Money, Power and Entitlement that institutions and people can set up to be self-reinforcing.

There have been a lot of recommendations regarding federal government reform and I — very intentionally — do not want to chase down all those rabbit holes and lose sight of the big picture.

Rather focus the Agenda on four core areas: representative-ness, visibility, performance, and reconception of the federal government as a portfolio enterprise.

Representative-ness is an intended basis of Congress and the President as they are tasked to work as a group to craft laws and policies. And while they represent a district, state-wide or national constituency, all are also expected to consider the national interest. In that spirit, I would propose the following:

- Introduce term limits for Congress (two terms for Senators, three terms for Representatives).
- Congress members should have mandatory face-to-face time with constituents and colleagues — meaning three weeks in Washington

DC (including bipartisan seating arrangements on the floor) and one week at home with pre-scheduled, required and open meetings with constituents.

- Conduct a comprehensive assessment as to how campaign funding impacts representative-ness — the key trade-off being the right to free speech vs whether or how funding impacts who can run and subsequent policy.
- Like the private sector, performance should matter. Warren Buffett's response to an interview in 2011 about making sitting members ineligible for re-election whenever the deficit exceeded 3% of GDP (or, I would add, if there's a government shut-down) was perhaps a tongue-in-cheek example, but self-regulation measures should be considered and implemented.

Representative-ness from the POV of reciprocity also means that common sense administrative rules must apply to federal officials. Whether it be responding to allegations of harassment, health insurance coverage, etc., representatives set the example and governance rules should be consistent with reasonable private sector best practices.

In the case for **visibility** and transparency, following the September 2011 attacks, a Republican administration increased the rate of classifying documents by 75% — largely on national security grounds.

The subsequent Democratic administration further took aim at both the press and government officials working with the press (in seeming contrast to the President stating the press "helps hold me accountable, helps hold our government accountable, and helps our democracy function"[31]).

---

[31] https://www.newyorker.com/magazine/2013/06/10/the-president-and-the-press

Michael Clemente, the executive vice president of Fox News, said ... that it was "downright chilling" that Mr. Rosen "was named a criminal co-conspirator for simply doing his job as a reporter." Bruce Brown, the executive director of the Reporters Committee for Freedom of the Press, added ... that treating "routine news-gathering efforts as evidence of criminality is extremely troubling and corrodes time-honored understandings between the public and the government about the role of the free press."

The Rosen case follows other signs that the administration has gone overboard in its zeal to find and muzzle insiders. The Associated Press revealed last week that the government had secretly seized two months' worth of records for telephones used by the agency's staff, partly to determine the source of a leak about a report involving a foiled terrorist plot in Yemen. At least two other major leak investigations are continuing. Six current and former administration officials have been indicted under the old Espionage Act for leaking classified information to the press and public. In 2010, a federal judge in Maryland sentenced a leaker to 20 months in jail while admitting that he was "in the dark as to the kind of documents" involved in the leak or what impact they had on national security.[32]

The trajectory continues into the current Republican administration with continued frustration with leaks — particularly during first half of 2017 including the June arrest of Reality Leigh Winner ...

> ... for violating federal law that prohibits the distribution of classified defense information.... In an FBI affidavit filed in federal court in Georgia on Monday, investigators allege Winner "printed and improperly removed classified intelligence reporting, which contained classified national defense information from an intelligence community agency, and unlawfully retained it." The affidavit claims Winner then passed along the information to an unidentified "online news outlet."[33]

---

[32] http://www.nytimes.com/2013/05/22/opinion/another-chilling-leak-investigation.html

> But the Justice Department announced Winner's arrest as The
> Intercept reported it had obtained a classified NSA report suggesting Russian
> hackers attacked a U.S. voting software supplier before last year's presidential
> election. The NSA report was dated May 5, the same as the document Winner
> is charged with leaking.[34]

There is a necessary tension between freedom of the press and the obligation
of those in an organization to hold secrets. The responsibility to get it right —
meaning verifying, calculating the value / risk, giving the government an
opportunity to respond or act as appropriate, etc. — lies with the press and
specifically the editorial staff.

We, the Public, obviously provide the final affirmation after publication, but
that tension will be there — and should be there.

But the effective crackdown needs to be re-considered.

Performance considers both policy-making and functional/operational.

In the context of policy-making, the concern ties to the capacity of Congress to
truly understand and work through issues which results in over-reliance on
lobbyists and departmental bureaucrats to, in effect, create policy.

> (In 2015) the Government Accountability Office (GAO) and the Congressional
> Research Service (CRS), which provide nonpartisan policy and program
> analysis to lawmakers, employ 20 percent fewer staffers than they did in 1979.
> The same pattern of diminished in-house expertise is true throughout
> government. As the University of Pennsylvania political scientist John DiIulio
> has noted, the number of federal bureaucrats declined about 10 percent

---

[33] https://www.theatlantic.com/politics/archive/2017/06/the-feds-arrest-a-alleged-leaker/529248/
[34] https://www.usatoday.com/story/news/politics/2017/09/28/accused-nsa-leaker-confession/715062001/

between 1984 and 2012. At the same time, business lobbying, political polarization, and wealth inequality all started their steady and unmitigated increases. Put simply, the pressures have increased. The ability of the government to deal with them has not....

With each passing year there are more products and services; there are new technologies; there is more relevant scientific knowledge. Take almost any subject matter—finance, medicine, any technology—and think what it would take to have an informed opinion about it now as opposed to in 1980.... In 2012, there were about 1.9 million articles published in 28,000 scholarly peer-reviewed academic journals. Most of those articles are available with a few clicks of a keyboard. But information is not knowledge, which requires a high level of training in the various disciplines of social science, along with a humanistic understanding of history and a good bit of experience....

The complexity of political demands is also increasing. The number of organizations with Washington representation more than doubled between 1981 and 2006, from 6,681 to 13,776. All of these organizations are in Washington for a reason: They have policies they'd like to see enacted and/or blocked, and they want to make those demands clear.... Lobbying expenditures have grown even more, from an estimated $200 million in 1983 to $3.24 billion in 2013—a sixfold increase, controlling for inflation. And this doesn't count the proliferation of strategic consulting and issues management and research organizations that now fill Washington....

There is also more legal complexity. The U.S. code of federal regulations grew from 71,224 pages in 1975 to 102,295 pages in 1980 to 174,545 pages by 2012. Some of this is the result of societal complexity—new technologies and new projects require new regulations. Some of it is the result of political demand complexity—many of the lobbying demands involve calls for new laws. And many of the laws are written in ways to obscure their impacts, adding a qualitative dimension to the complexity. This matters for a simple reason. To effectively make new law, one must understand existing law. To change existing law, one must understand existing law. The more expansive and complex the law, the more specialized knowledge it takes to become an expert. Government can invest in resources that would allow it to acquire this specialized knowledge, or it can rely on externally provided experts with a material stake to help it draft and enact laws. For decades, we have chosen the second.[35]

The lift here is two-fold:

- Elect representatives who have some area of expertise in pertinent areas (which lies with the electorate), and
- Right size funding for policy resources at the Congressional Budget Office, Government Accountability Office, and key staffers. You want to rotate staffers and responsibilities and carefully delineate responsibilities to offset risk of concentrating power behind the scenes, but, even without the proposal regarding term limits, more experienced and informed support structure seems appropriate.

Almost every president has entered the office speaking of improving operational performance and streamlining government but attention then shifts to other items that take precedence and focus slips into the background.

- Nominate a COO-type responsible for articulating and executing specific targets — and report on progress quarterly
- One specific area of focus would need to be culture — and re-orienting what is described as a civil service / bureaucratic / risk-averse culture towards more performance and outcome oriented

---

[35] https://www.theatlantic.com/politics/archive/2015/03/when-congress-cant

- Another starting point would be revisiting the General Accountability Office's annual report "Actions Needed to Reduce Fragmentation, Overlap, and Duplication and Achieve Other Financial Benefits"

Finally, **reconceive** the federal government as a portfolio enterprise which I see as an updated version of a conglomerate with a portfolio of focused / specific operational units (think both federal branches but also linking into state and local governments) — reporting into a relatively small, central management connected by a robust information architecture / data platform.

That information architecture needs to be structured in such a way that it easily 'tags' transactions, scrubs out to ensure privacy is maintained, but engineered to support data-based policies. The need isn't new — the Commission of Evidence-Based Policymaking recently highlighted importance "tackling the greatest problems facing evidence building today — data access is limited, privacy-protecting practices are inadequate, and the capacity to generate the evidence needed to support policy decisions is insufficient."[36]

Addressing the structural flaws in government — representative-ness, visibility, performance and reconception starts with the electorate setting a clear expectation — I am less bullish that the institution will easily self-correct — and supporting candidates accordingly.

While aspects draw on business principles to improve the organization, one needs to be ever-aware that government is distinctly not a business in its role as policy-maker and arbiter. Therefore, there is a deep need to hard code the controls and constraints and, occasionally, re-orient as circumstances change.

---

[36] https://www.cep.gov/content/dam/cep/report/cep-final-report.pdf

Deliberate. Act.

In their 2002 "Stealth Democracy," authors John Hibbing and Elizabeth Theiss-Morse highlighted two key — deeply held and intuitive — drivers at play in Americans' involvement in the political process:

- General aversion to politics and the political process

    The last thing people want is to be more involved in political decision making: They do not want to make political decisions themselves; they do not want to provide much input to those who are assigned to make these decisions; and they would rather not know all the details of the decision-making process. Most people have strong feelings on few if any of the issues the government needs to address and would much prefer to spend their time in nonpolitical pursuits....

    Participation in politics is low not because of the difficulty of registration requirements or the dearth of places for citizens to discuss politics, not because of the sometimes unseemly nature of debate in Congress or displeasure with a particular public policy. Participation in politics is low because people do not like politics even in the best of circumstances; in other words, they simply do not like the process of openly arriving at a decision in the face of diverse opinions. They do not like politics when they view it from afar and they certainly do not like politics when they participate in it themselves....

- Overcoming that aversion involves some emotional trigger typically grounded in unfairness or outrage:

    People's most intense desire for the political process is that it not take advantage of them by allowing certain entities such as special interests and elected officials to reap personal gains at the expense of ordinary people like themselves.... And rank-and-file Americans believe the existing structures of American politics allow ordinary people to be played for suckers. Their strongest and most earnest political goal is to get power away from self-serving politicians. But identifying who should not have power is easy; identifying who should have power is another story.... Not far behind "giving more power to selfish elites" on the list of disliked political procedures is "getting more personally involved." People indicate greater enthusiasm for more political involvement when popular democracy is presented as the only alternative to dominance by self-serving elites.

Play this out: the emotional trigger creates the energy and focus to draw the 'base' out for the election. Often, if successful, that energy disperses following the election during implementation — that tedious and drawn-out political process potentially clarifying what was intended, gaining agreement and going through the minutiae needed to draft policy. Leading, not surprisingly, to frustration, disillusionment, and a lack of outcomes.

We need to recognize the folly in this cycle and change the cycle itself.

And that, really, is what this book is about: a shifting the focus from identity politics towards outcome oriented.

The hard work of implementation is not going to go away — though we can streamline regulations — but we, the electorate, can and must set the tone at the front end — specifically electing representatives with constructive ideas on priority policy initiatives and the expectation of representing us through the process to achieve necessary outcomes.

The forward path in politics is not about forcing a broader population to engage in politics (ie direct democracy) but rather unknotting the aforementioned problem of "identifying who should have power."

Which is where pragmatism comes in.

Deliberately choosing to be pragmatic — meaning centered on outcomes and data and intentionally tuning out the hyperbole — is exactly that — a choice. It's choosing to be grounded and granular, to decide and get things done rather than adhering to a particular ideology or label.

Also, as mentioned in the structural reform section, there's a clear need for expertise in needed areas to reduce the potential impact of lobbyists and bureaucrats: experts in hot button issues need apply.

Which takes me back to this book.

This book is a declaration of what I believe we need to embrace to move forward.

It's a proposed political platform — grounded in Pragmatic Principles, US law as well as representative capitalism, reciprocity, and actuality — that does not fall into neat traditional buckets of Republican, Democrat, Conservative, Liberal, or what-not.

That outcome wasn't a contrived intentional process of including a bit of everything to find compromise. There is no carefully manicured stump speech. No focus groups (though, happily, some editors).

Similarly, potential political representatives should articulate their views on foundational assumptions, perceived priorities (and what they don't — not everything can be priority), how they handle the baked-in differences in point of view and approach to effectively manage a US$19+ trillion economy.

Avoid vacuous pleasantries and get to specifics.

We the People need to scratch at it enough, give the process enough attention, and ask the right questions to get a true measure not only of the policies but also the person underneath.

Lastly — although this book's focus is largely on the political arena, it's worth reiterating importance of pragmatism, reciprocity and actuality — with how we individually respond and how we interact with one another.

Less in circumstances that we agree or are homogenous — that's easy. But how we deal with differences and disagreements. That's the real measure.

Argue like you're right. Listen like you're wrong. Humility. Modesty. Kindness.

But, no matter what, it is about what **you** choose to do and how **you** choose to act.

This book is my act. Articulating another way. Deliberately pragmatic.

Thanks for reading.

Acknowledgements

Neither this book nor "Deliberate Performance" would have been written without Brene Brown's "Daring Greatly" — there is no way I would have committed my gremlins to writing and released them into the wild without that book.

As always, I am deeply thankful for — and humbled by — family and friends who support the process.

Thanks for the continued encouragement by Britt Hurley, Marjorie Balsham, Joana Burke, Mia Crespo, Pat Cook, Lorraine Davis, Jessica Drennan, Andrea DuCroiset, Susan Guarino, Marie Judge, Nicole Kitts, Stephanie Klem, Mora Melican, Jodie Patterson, Graham Scott, Kendall Thomas – immensely appreciated. My gremlins thank you.

To Rob Petti and my father – your thoughtful feedback is very much appreciated.

I am deeply indebted to (newly married) Laura Hinchy for her editorial guidance.

To my sons, Beck and Leo: this book is, to a large extent for you and your generation. We – meaning my generation and preceding ones – need to set a better example.

Most importantly to my wife, Irene. This is for you.

Appendix

Relevant excerpts taken from the U.S. Constitution

Article I. Section 7

All Bills for raising Revenue shall originate in the House of Representatives; but the Senate may propose or concur with Amendments as on other Bills.

Article I. Section 8

1: The Congress shall have Power To lay and collect Taxes, Duties, Imposts and Excises, to pay the Debts and provide for the common Defence and general Welfare of the United States; but all Duties, Imposts and Excises shall be uniform throughout the United States;

2: To borrow Money on the credit of the United States;

3: To regulate Commerce with foreign Nations, and among the several States, and with the Indian Tribes;

4: To establish an uniform Rule of Naturalization, and uniform Laws on the subject of Bankruptcies throughout the United States;

5: To coin Money, regulate the Value thereof, and of foreign Coin, and fix the Standard of Weights and Measures;

6: To provide for the Punishment of counterfeiting the Securities and current Coin of the United States;

7: To establish Post Offices and post Roads;

8: To promote the Progress of Science and useful Arts, by securing for limited Times to Authors and Inventors the exclusive Right to their respective Writings and Discoveries;

9: To constitute Tribunals inferior to the supreme Court;

10: To define and punish Piracies and Felonies committed on the high Seas, and Offences against the Law of Nations;

11: To declare War, grant Letters of Marque and Reprisal, and make Rules concerning Captures on Land and Water;

12: To raise and support Armies, but no Appropriation of Money to that Use shall be for a longer Term than two Years;

13: To provide and maintain a Navy;

14: To make Rules for the Government and Regulation of the land and naval Forces;

15: To provide for calling forth the Militia to execute the Laws of the Union, suppress Insurrections and repel Invasions;

16: To provide for organizing, arming, and disciplining, the Militia, and for governing such Part of them as may be employed in the Service of the United States, reserving to the States respectively, the Appointment of the Officers, and the Authority of training the Militia according to the discipline prescribed by Congress;

17: To exercise exclusive Legislation in all Cases whatsoever, over such District (not exceeding ten Miles square) as may, by Cession of particular States, and the Acceptance of Congress, become the Seat of the Government of the United States, and to exercise like Authority over all Places purchased by the Consent of the Legislature of the State in which the Same shall be, for the Erection of Forts, Magazines, Arsenals, dock-Yards, and other needful Buildings;—And

18: To make all Laws which shall be necessary and proper for carrying into Execution the foregoing Powers, and all other Powers vested by this Constitution in the Government of the United States, or in any Department or Officer thereof.

Article II. Section 2

1: The President shall be Commander in Chief of the Army and Navy of the United States, and of the Militia of the several States, when called into the actual Service of the United States; he may require the Opinion, in writing, of the principal Officer in each of the executive Departments, upon any Subject relating to the Duties of their respective Offices, and he shall have Power to grant Reprieves and Pardons for Offences against the United States, except in Cases of Impeachment.

2: He shall have Power, by and with the Advice and Consent of the Senate, to make Treaties, provided two thirds of the Senators present concur; and he shall nominate, and by and with the Advice and Consent of the Senate, shall appoint Ambassadors, other public Ministers and Consuls, Judges of the supreme Court, and all other Officers of the United States, whose Appointments are not herein otherwise provided for, and which shall be established by Law: but the Congress may by Law vest the Appointment of such inferior Officers, as they think proper, in the President alone, in the Courts of Law, or in the Heads of Departments.

Article V (Article 5 - Mode of Amendment)

The Congress, whenever two thirds of both Houses shall deem it necessary, shall propose Amendments to this Constitution, or, on the Application of the Legislatures of two thirds of the several States, shall call a Convention for proposing Amendments, which, in either Case, shall be valid to all Intents and Purposes, as Part of this Constitution, when ratified by the Legislatures of three fourths of the several States, or by Conventions in three fourths thereof, as the one or the other Mode of Ratification may be proposed by the Congress; Provided that no Amendment which may be made prior to the Year One thousand eight hundred and eight shall in any Manner affect the first and fourth Clauses in the Ninth Section of the first Article; and that no State, without its Consent, shall be deprived of its equal Suffrage in the Senate.

Bill of Rights

Article [I] (Amendment 1 - Freedom of expression and religion)

Congress shall make no law respecting an establishment of religion, or prohibiting the free exercise thereof; or abridging the freedom of speech, or of the press; or the right of the people peaceably to assemble, and to petition the Government for a redress of grievances.

Article [II] (Amendment 2 - Bearing Arms)

A well regulated Militia, being necessary to the security of a free State, the right of the people to keep and bear Arms, shall not be infringed.

Article III Conditions for quarters of soldiers

No soldier shall, in time of peace be quartered in any house, without the consent of the owner, nor in time of war, but in a manner to be prescribed by law.

Article IV Right of search and seizure regulated

The right of the people to be secure in their persons, houses, papers, and effects, against unreasonable searches and seizures, shall not be violated, and no warrants shall issue, but upon probable cause, supported by oath or affirmation, and particularly describing the place to be searched, and the persons or things to be seized. TOP

Article V Provisions concerning prosecution

No person shall be held to answer for a capital, or otherwise infamous crime, unless on a presentment or indictment of a Grand Jury, except in cases arising in the land or naval forces, or in the militia, when in actual service in time of war or public danger; nor shall any person be subject for the same offense to be twice put in jeopardy of life or limb; nor shall be compelled in any criminal case to be a witness against himself, nor be deprived of life, liberty, or property, without due process of law; nor shall private property be taken for public use without just compensation.

Article [X] (Amendment 10 - Reserved Powers)

The powers not delegated to the United States by the Constitution, nor prohibited by it to the States, are reserved to the States respectively, or to the people.

FORWARD: A PRAGMATIC AGENDA

Article XIV (Amendment 14 - Rights Guaranteed: Privileges and Immunities of Citizenship, Due Process, and Equal Protection)

1: All persons born or naturalized in the United States, and subject to the jurisdiction thereof, are citizens of the United States and of the State wherein they reside. No State shall make or enforce any law which shall abridge the privileges or immunities of citizens of the United States; nor shall any State deprive any person of life, liberty, or property, without due process of law; nor deny to any person within its jurisdiction the equal protection of the laws.

www.ingramcontent.com/pod-product-compliance
Lightning Source LLC
Chambersburg PA
CBHW060516280326
41933CB00014B/2984